OCEANS ALIVE

Sea Anemones

by Martha E. H. Rustad

BLASTOFF!
2
READERS

BELLWETHER MEDIA · MINNEAPOLIS, MN

Note to Librarians, Teachers, and Parents:

Blastoff! Readers are carefully developed by literacy experts and combine standards-based content with developmentally-appropriate text.

Level 1 provides the most support through repetition of high-frequency words, light text, predictable sentence patterns, and strong visual support.

Level 2 offers early readers a bit more challenge through varied simple sentences, increased text load, and less repetition of high frequency words.

Level 3 advances early-fluent readers toward fluency through increased text and concept load, less reliance on visuals, longer sentences, and more literary language.

Level 4 builds reading stamina by providing more text per page, increased use of punctuation, greater variation in sentence patterns, and increasingly challenging vocabulary.

Level 5 encourages children to move from "learning to read" to "reading to learn" by providing even more text, varied writing styles, and less familiar topics.

Whichever book is right for your reader, Blastoff! Readers are the perfect books to build confidence and encourage a love of reading that will last a lifetime!

This edition first published in 2008 by Bellwether Media.

No part of this publication may be reproduced in whole or in part without written permission of the publisher. For information regarding permission, write to Bellwether Media Inc., Attention: Permissions Department, Post Office Box 1C, Minnetonka, MN 55345-9998.

Library of Congress Cataloging-in-Publication Data
Rustad, Martha E. H. (Martha Elizabeth Hillman), 1975–
  Sea anemones / by Martha E.H. Rustad.
    p. cm. — (Blastoff! readers. Oceans alive)
Summary: "Simple text and supportive images introduce beginning readers to Sea Anemones. Intended for students in kindergarten through third grade"—Provided by publisher.
  Includes bibliographical references and index.
  ISBN-13: 978-1-60014-081-5 (hardcover : alk. paper)
  ISBN-10: 1-60014-081-5 (hardcover : alk. paper)
  1. Sea anemones—Juvenile literature. I. Title.
  QL377.C7R87 2008
  593.6—dc22   2007009797

Contents

Sea anemones are colorful ocean animals with long **tentacles**.

They have a soft body
shaped like a **tube**.

Sea anemones come in many sizes. Some are the size of your fingertip.

Some are bigger than
a person.

Sea anemones live on the
ocean floor. They live on rock
or **coral**.

Sea anemones grip tightly
onto rock or coral.

Some sea anemones live in **tide pools**. Water goes in and out of tide pools each day.

Sea anemones pull in their
tentacles when the water goes
out. Their bodies stay wet inside.

Some big fish try to eat
sea anemones.

Sea anemones can **sting** fish with their tentacles. The tentacles hold **poison**.

13

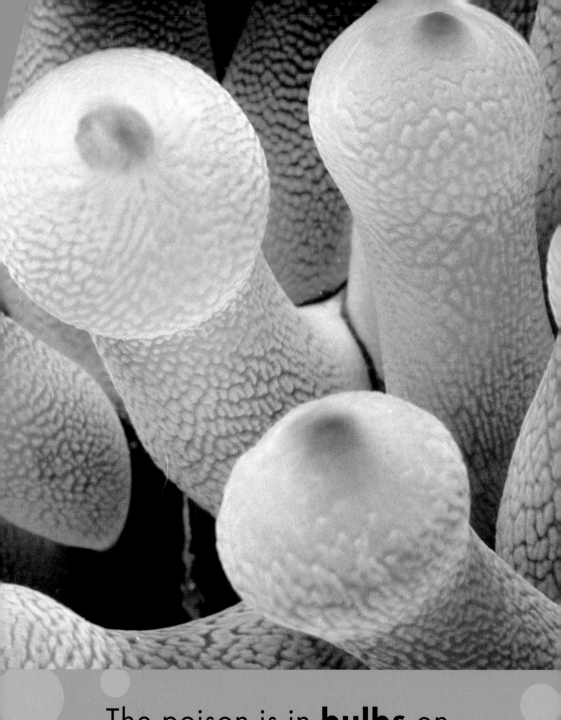

The poison is in **bulbs** on the end of the tentacles.

Not all sea anemone tentacles look the same. Some tentacles are long and thin.

15

Some tentacles are short
and thick.

Sea anemones sting small fish
for food. Their tentacles push
the food into their mouths.

17

mouth

Their mouth is at the top of their body.

Not all fish can be stung by
sea anemones.

Clown fish are protected from stings by **slime** on their bodies.

Sea anemones protect
clown fish from other fish.

Glossary

bulb—a round part near the end of sea anemone tentacles that holds poison

coral—an ocean animal that forms a hard skeleton around parts of its body

poison—a material that can hurt or kill another living thing

slime—a clear, slippery liquid that covers the body of a clown fish

sting—to hurt with a sharp, poisoned body part

tentacle—a thin, flexible body part; sea anemones have many tentacles.

tide pool—a pool of water that stays near the shore when the tide goes out

tube—a long, hollow shape; a tube is shaped like a straw or a pipe.

To Learn More

AT THE LIBRARY

Cole, Melissa. *Coral Reefs*. Farmington Hills, Mich.: Blackbirch Press, 2004.

Schaefer, Lola M. *Sea Anemones*. Chicago, Ill.: Heinemann Library, 2002.

Stone, Lynn M. *Sea Anemones*. Vero Beach, Fla.: Rourke, 2003.

Whitehouse, Patricia. *Hiding in a Coral Reef*. Chicago, Ill.: Heinemann Library, 2003.

ON THE WEB

Learning more about sea anemones is as easy as 1, 2, 3.

1. Go to www.factsurfer.com

2. Enter "sea anemones" into search box.

3. Click the "Surf" button and you will see a list of related web sites.

With factsurfer.com, finding more information is just a click away.

Index

The photographs in this book are reproduced through the courtesy of: George Grall/Getty Images, front cover; Chris Newbert/Minden Pictures, pp. 4-5; Brian J Skerry/Getty Images, p. 6; Image State/Alamyp. 7; Stuart Westmorland/Age fotostock, p. 8; Marevision/Age fotostock, pp. 9, 17; Georgette Douwma/Getty Images, pp. 10-11; Michael Patrick O'Neill/Alamy, pp. 12-13; Norbert Wu/Getty Images, p. 14; Robert Dalton, p. 15; Mark Conlin/V&W/imagequestmarine.com, p. 16; Brandon Cole Marine Photography/Alamy, p. 18; Jeff Foott/Getty Images, p. 19; Jeff Hunter/Getty Images, pp. 20-21.